Rest for the Weary Soul

ISBN: 978-1-957262-95-6
Rest for the Weary Soul

Copyright © 2023 by Marina Murray
All rights reserved.

No part of this publication may be reproduced, distributed, or transmitted in any form or by any means, including photocopying, recording, or other electronic or mechanical methods, without the prior written permission of the publisher, except in the case of brief quotations embodied in critical reviews and certain other noncommercial uses permitted by copyright law.

For permission requests, write to the publisher at the address below.

Yorkshire Publishing
1425 E 41st Pl
Tulsa, OK 74105
www.YorkshirePublishing.com
918.394.2665

Published in the USA

Rest for the Weary Soul

Marina Murray

My intention in writing this book is to encourage you in your walk with God. In this life there are so many trials, problems, and hardships that will knock you down. I hope that these words encourage and strengthen you to stand back up again. Life's problems will come and go but God always stays.

-Marina Murray

CONTENTS

Who is God 9	Know Him More......................35
Blessed by You..........................11	He Changes Us 37
Holy Spirit 13	Master Craftsman......................38
I Trust You 14	Child of The Most High 39
Master of My Heart...................15	Trust God...................................41
The Great Shepherd 17	Something Better in Mind........45
My Provider 19	Not My Way 47
Jehovah Shammah.....................20	Lead Me.....................................50
The Great Warrior.....................21	Lead the Way 51
Nothing that You Can't Do 22	Blood Bought............................52
Prince of Peace 24	Set Me Free 53
Jehovah Jireh 25	Choose Him Too.......................55
When He Calls..........................26	His Cherished Creation.............59
How to Pray..............................28	I Trust Your Plan 61
Made Whole 30	Beauty in Our Pain 63
His Word Renews.....................32	Forgiveness................................64
He Changed My Mind..............33	Love Him First..........................65

Unfailing Love..............................67	My Greatest Love 76
Sold Out 68	I Love You 77
Reason to Boast...........................70	Crush on You 78
My Soul's Desire..........................71	Seeker of Souls 79
Glorify You..................................72	My Everything 81
Praise You from the floor............73	The Lamb 82
Glorify Your Name.....................74	

Who is God

You are the creator of the universe, and You created everything that inhabits it. With love, You created every human, plant, and animal. You are my God, my heavenly father, my provider, my master, and my friend. Your names are great and worthy of praise. Your names reveal Your nature. You are Jehovah Jireh, the God who provides. You are Jehovah Shalom, the perfect peace amid the storm. You are Jehovah Shammah—the one who is always present. You promised never to leave me nor forsake me. You are with me every moment. You are Jehovah Rapha—the one who heals the body, mind, and soul. There is no sickness too great for You to heal. You are Jehovah Sabaoth, the mighty warrior who fights for me. You are Jehovah Nissi; You are my victory. You are Yahweh Tsidkenu; You are my righteousness. As I remember Your names, my fears and doubts fade away. If God is for me, who can be against me? You are God almighty, and You never fail, so I put my hope and trust in You.

Blessed by You

I am so blessed by You

There is so much that You do

You provide for my needs

It's Your name that every enemy heeds

You conquered them all

You promised never to let me fall

You are always by my side

Forever, you'll be my guide

You quiet my racing thoughts and give me peace

You make every enemy cease

You protect me each day

You have the final say

You're the healer of my soul

You made me whole

You forgive every sin

You're the God that will always win

You're mighty and full of grace

Marina Murray

Nothing could take your place

You're greater than them all

Forever I'll listen to Your call

I want to be led by You

You're perfect in all that You do

There's no one like You

Holy Spirit

You are a gentleman. You are the one who came when our savior, Jesus, ascended into Heaven. You are the gentle, quiet spirit that whispers in my ear. You encourage me to do what is right and lovingly correct me when I am wrong. You never let your kind, gentle spirit overpower my choices and decisions. As a gentleman, you give me the option to either follow you or go astray. You provide me with life, fulfillment, and joy, making it easy for me to follow you. You interceded on my behalf and led me down the path of life. You put a song in my heart and joy in my soul. I am grateful for your presence and your spirit guiding me home.

I Trust You

I feel Your hand upon my life. You're the gentle voice that leads the way. You bless me in every season, and You are present during every trial. You give me victory and healing in my heart. Your instructions are simple, which is to trust and obey. I listen to God, who has the final say. You give me peace and joy. You put a song in my heart. Your love is perfect, unfailing, and pure. You immerse me with love and lead the way. My God, I will always trust and obey You.

Master of My Heart

My God, I love You so much

You're always in touch

You understand every problem and need

Your faithfulness has nothing to do with a good or

bad deed

You always provide for me

You loved me enough to set me free

I can never repay my debt to You

Forever I'll sing and glorify all that You do

Thank You for forgiving me

Thank You for setting me free

Thank You for Your love, mercy, and grace

You are with me in every place

Thank You for loving me in my worst state

You have forever changed my fate

You love me even when I miss the mark

You're with me even when this world feels dark

Marina Murray

Your name is forever carved upon my heart

From You, I'll never part

You loved me from the start

You'll forever own my heart

The Great Shepherd

You look after me like a shepherd looks after a sheep that has gone astray. You search high and low. You knock on the door to my heart, longing for me to let you in. You hold the lamp that lights the path for my feet. You are the rock that I cling to. You are the kind, loving father who welcomes me home with open arms. You watch over me as I sleep. You give me every breath that I take. When I cry, You are the big strong arms that wrap around me and surround me with love. You saw me and loved me. You see the imperfections, flaws, sins, and depths of my soul, and You still choose to love me. You sent Your son Jesus to carry my cross. With His blood, You washed me clean. I could never earn Your love with good works or good deeds. I could never do enough to earn Your perfect, unfailing love. It is through Christ that I have been redeemed. Who am I that You would send Your one and only son to die for me? Your love for me is so great I will never truly understand it. You are my shepherd, the one who leads the way. Though I stumble, I will never fall, for it is You who holds my hand.

My Provider

When I worry that I won't have enough or dwell upon what I need but can't afford, I cry out to the Lord. He reminds me that He will not leave me nor forsake me. He reminds me that He will provide for my every need. So, I cast my cares upon Him and remain obedient with my tithe. The Lord loves a cheerful giver; as I choose to give, I do it joyfully because I know He will provide for my every need; I need to trust and obey His word. It is He that makes me lie down in green pastures. The Lord is my shepherd; I will never be in need because He always provides.

Marina Murray

Jehovah Shammah

You are loyal, and You stick by my side

You will forever be my guide

You're present through every trial,

heartbreak, and victory

Your love is a mystery

Each day You hold my hand

Your love is so grand

And give me the strength to withstand it all

You promised not to let me fall

I will never be in fear

Because I know that You're near

You're the friend that travels by my side

In You, I'll trust and abide

The Great Warrior

This battle feels impossible. I have fought with all of my strength and all of my might, but nothing has happened. I cry out to the Lord, Jehovah Sabaoth. The battle is not to be fought with fists, weapons, or clever words. This battle that wages on is not between flesh and blood but between rulers and principalities. This battle is to be fought with my hands and knees in prayer. It is fought by singing His praise, reading His word, fasting, trusting in Him, and putting on the armor of God. I rejoice because I serve a God that cannot fail. My God is great, mighty, and has already won. The battle was won at the cross, so I lift my hands and praise His great name.

Marina Murray

Nothing that You Can't Do

I fall on my knees in prayer

My heart breaks because this is not fair

I can't do this on my own

The weight of my burden breaks every bone

My heart is so broken inside

I can't run or hide

I'm overwhelmed with grief

I am in disbelief

I am broken far beneath the surface of my skin

You're the God who will always win

My heart is troubled, and my mind is in a race

Tears cover my face

I cast my cares at your feet

There is no enemy that You can't beat

You quiet every racing thought in my mind

You're so loving and kind

You give me great peace in my heart

You shield me from every weapon and fiery dart

My hope and trust is in You

There's nothing that You can't do

Marina Murray

Prince of Peace

When I feel hopeless, trapped, alone, and as though nothing will get better, You take me by the hand and remind me that You will never leave me nor forsake me. You are with me every step of the way. Though my battle feels impossible and greater than I can bear. God reminds me that I am not alone. He reminds me that I am a conqueror through Christ, who strengthens me. He tells me to cast my cares upon Him, and He will fight these battles for me. Even though I feel weak, He is strong. His strength is made perfect through my weakness. My troubled heart is quieted as Jehovah Shalom's perfect peace surrounds me.

Jehovah Jireh

You are The One who provides. You provide food for the birds. You clothe every flower in beauty. You provide for every creature; even though they don't serve You or praise Your name, You still provide for their every need. So, how much greater is Your promise to provide for me? I will not worry about what to eat, what to drink, or what I will wear, for I know that You will provide for my every need. You are my provider, so I put my hope and trust in You. I never walk away from You empty-handed because You are my loving heavenly father, who provides for my every need. You are mighty and worthy of every praise.

When He Calls

When God is moving and working in your life, you might not necessarily see divine intervention. God may not physically part the sea in front of you, but He will put people in your life to help you in the specific season you're in. These people may say the words that you need to hear to help you when you're in a specific circumstance. God uses people to do His will. God helps you every day, and you need to learn how to hear His voice. Stop trying to fix or figure it all out on your own; just pray, and call out to God for help. He will make a way for you. He is waiting patiently for you to call out to Him for help. He doesn't want you to do or fix it all by yourself. Call upon God; He knows exactly what you need. When God speaks to you, listen and respond because He uses you to help others. His calling may not be an audible voice, it may feel like a suggestion or thought, or it could be "just a feeling." These aren't your thoughts or ideas; this is God calling upon you and instructing you to help. So, don't ignore this call because just like God uses people to help you, He will use you to help others. These callings from God may not be huge or grand acts. It could be giving a stranger a word of encouragement, a feeling or strong desire to check on someone, etc. God uses us all to fulfill His will. So, listen to His call, and don't be afraid to call out to Him for help. He's waiting to hear from you.

Marina Murray

How to Pray

God hates vain repetition

Our prayers aren't a competition

You don't need pretty words or fancy speech

He is not beyond your reach

I'll tell you how to start

Make sure your words come from your heart

If you really don't know what to say

Start by telling Him about your day

It's God; he already knows

But it is better than empty words dressed in bows

Be honest; just tell God how you feel

It's not a big deal

He's your father, and He wants to know

You don't need to put on a show

He is waiting to hear from you

There's nothing special that you need to do

He loves you so much

Don't worry; He's not out of touch

He knows about your problems and your needs

And all of your good and bad deeds

His love is greater than you can understand

Don't worry; He'll hold your hand

I know that you're nervous, so here's what to say

Start by telling Him about your day

Made Whole

Jesus paid the price for every sin. God knew every sin that each of us would commit; He knew about this before He even created us. So, God asked His one and only son to die in our place. God asked Jesus to sacrifice himself for our sins. Every injury, wound, and every part of Jesus' body that was broken was done to pay the price for every sin, even those that haven't been committed yet. Jesus paid for it all, even before we were even born. The horrifically broken pieces of Jesus' body were an external, tangible expression of our sins. Jesus wears the scars of our sins on His body every day for everyone to see. This is not to shame us or to make us feel guilty. It's to help us to understand how much He loves us. Jesus is a perfect, spotless, and blameless being. His body was whole and perfect.

Jesus chose to sacrifice himself for our sins. He decided to take our sins on his body and to take on our guilt and shame so that we don't have to. He took our sins out of love for us because God did not want us to be broken like this. God did not want us to die and suffer for our sins. God chose to come to earth in a human form (Jesus) so that He could give us an example to live our lives by, and then He became the perfect sacrifice so that we could be set free from our sins and saved from Hell. When we die and go to Heaven, we get new bodies, perfect ones, healed and whole, but Jesus' body bears the marks that paid the price for the purchase of mankind. Jesus paid the price of our sins, so that we never have to. He sacrificed himself so that we can be made whole and new.

His Word Renews

Open your bible and read for a while

I'm sure that it will make you smile

It's one thing that's worth your while

When you do,

You'll see that He will make you new

He changed me from the start

I know that you can't see my heart

But He changed it and made it new

There is nothing that He can't do

I thought that it was broken beyond repair

But He fixed it because He does care

His words are loving and kind

He has an answer for every bind

So let Him change your mind

Get away from the daily grind

He has a word just for you

He loves you, and you'll love Him too

He Changed My Mind

He made me new

Now there are things that I simply won't do

He didn't change my body, but He changed my heart

That's where all things start

Then He changed my mind

He made me more patient and kind

He changes me more each day

He'll keep working until the old me is stripped away

Every day I love Him more

He keeps opening a new door

One that leads to life, salvation, and joy

Life with Him is easy to enjoy

Even when my life feels off track

I never want to go back

To the life that I lived before

Now He opened another door

His love is something to explore

Life with Him is never a bore

Give Him a chance to change your mind

I bet that He will make you more patient and kind

You'll never want to go astray

With Him, you'll always stay

Know Him More

God does not leave us when we sin. He still loves us and desires us to turn away from our sins and come to Him. None of us are perfect; we all sin. However, we should not make it a habit. Sin separates us from God because it is imperfect and unholy. God is a perfect, holy being, and He cannot be in the presence of sin. God does not ever want to be separated from us, and that's why He called His son to become the sacrifice for our sins. Turning away from sin (repenting) allows us to be in the presence of God, and it allows us to be close to Him. God does not want us to be focused on being perfect or fulfilling religious duties. God detests meaningless repetitive rituals and traditions. God looks at our heart, this is what matters most to Him. If our heart is not a part of our actions, words, ceremonies, etc., it is meaningless to God. His desire for us is to have a relationship with

Him. He wants us to get to know Him by reading and applying His word to our daily lives and by spending time in prayer and worshiping Him.

He Changes Us

When Jesus enters our lives, change begins

He strips away all of our sins

It happens by the power of His might.

We are all precious in His sight

When we read our Bible, it speaks to our soul

It softens our hearts, isn't that the goal?

To be more like Christ and love like Him too

His love is special; it sticks tighter than glue

You don't have to be perfect to fit in

Jesus still loves us, even though we all sin

As we grow in Christ, our behavior changes too

Because He makes us new

We become more loving and kind

I am sure that your family won't mind

To be around the better version of you

I'm sure that you'll like it too

Master Craftsman

God rejuvenates my soul. He brings life back to what I thought was dead. He restores the things that I thought I had lost. He heals the broken pieces of my heart. As I surrender to Him, He takes the rough, jagged, ugly pieces of my life, and He sands them down, smooths them, and creates something beautiful. There is nothing that He can't restore. There is nothing that He can't fix. There is nothing that He can't make beautiful. I watch in awe as He restores the broken pieces of my life and soul that I have surrendered to Him. He restores and perfects everything, so I quickly surrender all that I am, and I have to You, Lord, for You make all things beautiful.

Child of The Most High

I fall to my knees

My heart breaks and bleeds

I feel so broken inside

I begin to cry

God, I need You more than You know

I feel so alone

I can't do this on my own

I need Your help

Please show me Your way

I don't have pretty words to pray

But please, hear my cry

My heart hurts so much inside

I feel Your presence surrounding me

You wipe the tears from my eyes

And remind me that You never left my side

You hold me in Your arms and say that it will be ok

You whisper in my ear

Marina Murray

That I am a child of The Most High God

So, I have nothing to fear

You take me by the hand and lead the way

I am so thankful that You're with me night and day

Trust God

It is foolish to distrust God. We think that because God didn't answer a specific prayer, He doesn't have our best interests in mind, or we begin to doubt His word. God is not a genie; He doesn't answer every wish we have. The reason is that God has our best interests in mind. Just because we don't get the house, car, or job does not mean God doesn't care. God just has something better in mind. God is trying to protect you when He says no. People get mad at God and blame Him for their problems, even though they are not His fault. People blame God for the death of their loved ones. God did not need another angel in heaven; that's not why your loved one died. The moment Adam and Eve ate from the tree of good and evil, sin entered this world, and that's why we have sickness and disease. God never intended for us to live our lives this way. Your loved one didn't die because God needed another angel. If God wanted another angel, God would have made one. This is the God that spoke light into existence. He does not need to take your loved one to become an angel. God doesn't turn us into angels when we die. When we die and go to Heaven, He gives us new bodies that are perfect and whole. This life is temporary, and God is giving us a choice to accept Jesus and serve God or not. We get so focused on the tangible things of this world, like money, houses, cars, etc. These are not bad things, but they should not be our primary focus. Set your focus on God, and then everything else will fall into place. God is the one that created the world. He created everything in it, even the gold and the trees that we use to print our paper money, and He created every resource that we have. Everything on this Earth is temporary. So, don't get caught up in trying to keep up with the Jones. The money won't last, the car will rust, and the house can crumble.

The treasures of this world don't last. So, store up your treasures in heaven. You do this by feeding the poor, helping your neighbor, and sharing your wealth, and serving others. If you don't have money to give, give your time. Pray for people, help people, encourage people, and share the word of God. God called us to love others; He did not call us to make a bunch of money and then die. Share what you have, love others, be kind to each other, and share the mercy and grace that God has given to you and the people that you encounter. This is how you store up treasures in Heaven. The treasures in Heaven don't break, rust, and can't be taken away. So, when God says no, or doesn't answer your prayer, just know it is because God has something better in mind for you. You may not see it today or tomorrow, but God truly has your best interests in mind. God's loving thoughts for you each day outnumber the grains of sand on the shore. The second that we doubt God is when the devil tries to tempt us with sin. That's how he tricked Adam and Eve in the garden of Eden. Satan made them question whether or not God had their best interests in mind. Adam and Eve took the devil's bait because they questioned and then doubted God. So, read your Bible daily to bury God's words and His truth deep within your heart. So, when the devil starts to sow seeds of doubt in your mind and make you question or doubt God, you remember the truth. Set your eyes on the prize. When you set your eyes and focus upon God, your life will be fulfilled; you will be satisfied, and you will have peace and joy in the middle of the storm. God loves us more than we can ever know. So, don't let Satan allow you to doubt God. Always put your faith and trust in God.

Something Better in Mind

I don't understand why I don't get my way

I pray every night and every day

It seems like You don't listen to my prayers

Aren't You the God who cares

My heart is breaking, and I don't understand

Why is it that the God that's so grand,

Won't help me when I am in my time of need

My heart begins to break and bleed

God, please, I don't understand

You're the God that holds the world in Your hand

Why don't you answer my prayer

This is so unfair

You look at me and shake Your head

And ask if it is Your word that I have read

You promised to provide for my every need

It has nothing to do with a good or bad deed

This simply is not Your will for me

Marina Murray

I don't always see

That You have something better in mind

I begin to relax and unwind

I may not always get my way

But You're still with me, night and day

Not My Way

My God, why didn't I get that house

I prayed every day, but You were as silent as a mouse

I also never got that job

Are my dreams created for You to rob

You are silent to every prayer

None of this is fair

I read my Bible and pray

Isn't that what the pastors say

I try to get to know You more

But You shut every door

Nothing seems to go right

Am I actually precious in Your sight

You crush all of my hopes and dreams

Your love isn't what it seems

Why is it me that You want to smite

You shake Your head and tell me

that my thinking isn't right

You have something better in mind

Your actions are kind

You have great plans for me

I just can't see

You look far ahead

That's why I need to be led

I can't see the entire way

Sometimes I struggle day to day

You remind me that it's good to pray

Sometimes I need to let go

It's a blessing when You say no

Your plans are better than mine

Everything will be fine

You're the one who knows it all

You promised not to let me fall

You have my best interests in mind

You've gotten me out of every bind

It's hard when I don't get my way

But it's with You that I'll always stay

Rest for the Weary Soul

Your plans are greater than I understand

So, I hold out my hand

Trusting in your greater plan

Please lead me in Your way

For You are with me night and day

Lead Me

There are days that I doubt You, days that I question whether You are enough. Whether I should take my own path or make my own way. But who am I, the creation, to question the creator? You created the laws that nature follows. You are the God who was, is, and always will be. How foolish is it for me to question You? I could spend my entire life learning and studying and still never understand how You put the stars in the sky. Or how You created the rhythms and laws that Your creations follow. So, I choose to surrender to You. I choose to trust You. I choose to be led by You. You are far greater, smarter, stronger, and wiser than I am, so I choose to trust You. I choose to submit to You and to obey Your word, for it is good.

Lead the Way

God is perfect, and so is His love

His love fits just like a glove

It never changes or fails

His love always prevails

Aren't you tired of chasing your tails

Going in circles, and everything fails

Why do you make a different path

Are you trying to give us all a good laugh

He already paved the way

He is with you night and day

Trust in Him, and He'll lead the way

With Him, I'll always stay

Blood Bought

With His blood, He bought us to set us free. That price is greater than silver and gold; its value is higher than any commodity. The God who created the universe loved you enough to pay the price of your freedom. With love, He laid His life down to set you free. You never have to pay the price for your own sins, bear the burden, or wear the yoke of bondage of sin because Jesus did that for you. His love for you is so great; He even gives you a choice. Every day we are given the option to follow Him or to go astray. He loves you so much that He never forces you to choose Him. He gave you free will so that you can have a say.

Set Me Free

Jesus paid the price to save me and make me new

There is nothing that He can't do

You broke my shackles and chains

Now I jump for joy, even when it rains

You set me free

I praise and shout with glee

Wake up, everyone. Come with me

Don't you see that He can set you free?

Free to love and free to dance

That devil doesn't stand a chance

He defeated shame, guilt, and sin

Jesus will always win

He did it not to boast

But because He loves us the most

Wake up, don't you see

That His love isn't just for me

He loves you more than you can know

Marina Murray

I'm sure that will make your heart glow

Shout it out loud so that everyone will see

That Jesus set the captives free

He took my burdens from me

Now that weight is gone, I see

How much He really loves me

His love is free

Shout and wake up the dead

Make sure that everyone has read

About His unfailing love

That comes from above

Choose Him Too

Surrendering to God does not mean that you're weak, simple-minded, or naive. Choosing to surrender to God is very wise. God is the one who knows all things. God knows every secret, every minor detail. He knows about every large and complex issue as well. The God that created the universe also created us. He put the stars in the sky and the freckles on your cheeks. He created every major thing and every minor detail. When you surrender to the all-knowing God, you're saying; I don't know everything, and I need God; I am not perfect, but God is, I don't have the answers, but God does. After surrendering to God, we need to obey His word because God gave us His word for a reason. His word is written in the Bible. The Bible is not an old book filled with dead words. The Bible is God's instruction on how to live our lives. It's filled with parables because not every problem has a black-and-white answer. But when you read the Bible, you're reading the instruction manual for how to live a successful and prosperous life. God created each one of us with a unique purpose and design. Everybody was designed to work together to help each other and bring glory to the God who created us. Each one of us is a masterpiece that was created by the hands of God. We were all created unique and different for a reason. The beauty in that is that we are all these beautiful masterpieces that are uniquely different. When we all work towards our purpose, it brings us all together, we are interconnected, and our uniqueness creates something beautiful. This complex, interconnected beauty brings glory to God. Our interconnected complex beauty glorifies God because it reflects who He is. He also created the Earth and universe this way. The earth sits in space and rotates on an axis that allows for seasons. Plants, animals, and natural occurrences thrive every season, which is crucial for survival. Each season uniquely differs from the others, but each one is important and beautiful. The winter is full of cold, snowy days and hot cocoa, sledding, ice skating, skiing, snowboarding, ice fishing, snowball fights, etc. In the spring, everything comes back to life. The birds chirp and sing, the flowers bloom, and we ditch our heavy winter coats. In the summer we go swimming, sun tan, there are concerts and festivals. Fall is when everything gets cold and starts to die and change colors. That's when we pick apples, drink apple cider, and harvest our crops. The point is that in every season, there is something to enjoy. Each season is uniquely different, but that is part of its beauty. These changes in season are more than just a change in the temperature; these seasons help us know when to plant and harvest our crops. Certain things die and change to prevent overgrowth or scarcities. The delicate interconnected balance sustains us and allows us to grow and flourish.

God made everything so complex, unique, and interconnected that it can bring Him glory. It reflects who He is. So, surrendering to a God like this is one of the wisest things that we can do. I may not have all the answers, I can't solve all the problems, and I can't control every outcome, but I serve a God who does. I surrender to Him because I trust and love Him. He has every answer. He is kind, loving, and can bless you. He will pour out His unfailing, perfect love upon you. He does not force us to surrender, and He does not force us to obey. He loves and chooses us daily, so He wants us to love and choose Him too.

His Cherished Creation

Looking in the mirror, I hate what looks back at me. I feel ugly and imperfect in every way. I know that I always fall short. As I stare into the mirror with red tear-stained eyes, You remind me that I was made in Your image. I was knit together in my mother's womb by You. You, my God, are perfect, without fault, and You do not make mistakes. With Your hands, You molded and shaped me like clay. You numbered the hairs upon my head. You call me beautiful, You call me Yours, and You made me in Your image. You call me redeemed. You love me more than I can ever understand. You look at me with Your loving eyes, see my imperfections and flaws, and tell me that they are perfect in Your sight. You wipe the tears from my eyes and tell me I am loved, beautiful, and Your cherished creation. You loved me first, and Your love never fails. You have made me perfect for your purpose and plan for my life. Your plan is good. Your plan is to give me hope and a future.

I Trust Your Plan

I kneel before You

Surrendering to You is what I choose to do

I trust Your plan

You're wiser than any man

You're perfect and good

Anyone with wisdom should

Submit to You

It's the best thing to do

Thank you for Your peace and grace

It gives me the strength to face

Another day

Because You have the final say

Please, God, lead the way

I will obey

It is You that I desire

It's Your love that I admire

I'll do as You say

Please, God, lead the way

Beauty in Our Pain

God doesn't cause bad things to happen to us. He doesn't want to hurt us. When we forgive, and we surrender the burdens of our pain to Him, He takes it and creates something beautiful. So, don't cling to your pain; forgive, and give it to God so He can transform it into something beautiful.

Forgiveness

Forgiveness is not easy, and it is not fun

But God, don't You see all that they have done

You tell me to pray for those who persecute me

But my God, don't you see

This is not easy to do

You want me to feed and bless them too

You say to conquer evil by doing good

Alright, I know that I should

I'll trust You and abide

I know that You're on my side

Forgiveness was really for me

I was blind, but now I see

To heal, I need to let go

I won't take revenge upon my foe

Why didn't I see

I really need to forgive because You forgave me

Love Him First

The love that we desperately desire is not a man or woman's love, it's from God. That is why we have such disappointment in our relationships. The love in every sappy chick flick, love song, or story is the unfailing, sacrificial love that only comes from God. Human love is not unfailing, it's beautiful, and we can only love because God loved us first. However, when we don't understand this and make a man or a woman responsible for this type of love that we feel is missing within our soul, we set our relationships up for failure because that is not what these people were meant to be. God desires us to love each other and to be kind, loving, patient, and forgiving with our spouses. However, these are not the answers to the empty spot in our hearts that longs for and desires beautiful, perfect, spotless, unfailing love. That type of love only comes from God. He alone is meant to love us this way. The unfulfillment that we feel is not because of our partner and their flaws but because we are trying to make them stretch and fit into a big hole to satisfy a great hunger that they weren't meant to fulfill. To find the joy that you need and to satisfy the desire in your soul, you need to first fill yourself up with God, His love, and let Him fill the empty, broken spot in your heart; then, you will be able to love your spouse the way that God intended.

God comes first; we are to love Him more than anything and anyone else. After doing this, we can love others more and become the husband or wife God has called us to be.

Unfailing Love

It is God's unfailing love that heals and holds the broken pieces of my heart. It is His words that soothe the depths of my soul. It is His presence that quiets my racing thoughts and brings me peace. In a world that feels lost and broken, it is His promises that I cling to because I have a desperate desire deep within my soul that longs for Him more and more each day. When my heart feels troubled and deeply overwhelmed, God wraps His loving arms around me and holds me close.

Sold Out

My greatest hope and desire is that more people will learn to love God with all their strength, might, and soul. Once this happens, your life will never be the same. You will grow in wisdom, understanding, and discernment. Your life will be completely and utterly changed. You will be filled with joy. Your problems won't disappear, but you'll have peace in the middle of the storm. You will be able to love others more deeply. You will lose your desire to please people, and you'll desire to please God. Your soul will just sing for God. You will have so much joy in your soul that it makes no sense. You will be in the middle of pure chaos and feel at peace, and you'll have joy, and people will look at you like you're clueless about your circumstance. They will wonder what you're on because your peace won't make sense. You'll still be sad at times, you'll still get your heart broken, or have times where you have stress, but it won't look like everyone else's because your peace and joy are unshakeable, and your faith is rooted in God. You'll be walking by faith, not by sight. When you remember the promises of God, you'll have nothing to fear. When you switch from pleasing people to pleasing God, your life will truly be transformed; you will be completely sold out to God. This is the best way to live because our purpose is to please, serve, and worship Him. Let yourself become wholly sold out to Him, and watch how He'll move; your life will never be the same.

Reason to Boast

I'm about to name-drop and boast

Because I know God, Jesus, and the Holy Ghost

They're the ones who love you the most

If you don't know them, you're toast

So don't be idle and coast

Be careful about who you host

If you listen to the devil, you'll roast

That's what Satan wants the most

For you to sit in Hell, so he can boast

About stealing you away from the

one who loves you the most

So, listen to the Holy Ghost

He'll give you a reason to boast

Because he'll lead you to the one

who loves you the most

My Soul's Desire

When my legs feel weary, and my burdens feel greater than I can bear, I will lean on You, Lord. When my heart feels broken beyond repair, I cry out to You because I know You care. When my soul is wounded and in despair. Lead me, God, in the way that only You can. When the burdens of this life crush me, and I feel like I can't stand, You carry me in Your arms. You put my feet on solid ground, and Your words restore my soul. I cry out to You like a child calls out for their parent to rescue them. You, God, are my rescuer, redeemer, protector, and friend. My soul desires You. When I am sad, my soul cries out to You. When I am happy, my soul sings to You. Despite my struggles, joy, and pain, the only thing that remains the same is You. I will always love You, and my soul will always sing Your praise.

Marina Murray

Glorify You

You're perfect and full of love

You shower Your mercy and grace from above

Immerse me in You

Please tell me what to do

So that I can please You more

I will feed and bless the poor

I will do whatever You say

Even though it is hard, I will trust You and obey

I want to bring honor and glory to Your name

You took my burdens and shame

I can't get enough of You

I'll praise You until my face turns blue

To You, I surrender it all

You catch me when I fall

My God, please tell me what to do

So that I can glorify You

Praise You from the floor

Praise is how I get close to You

It's something that I'll always do

What an honor to be in the presence of the Lord

Even in silence, I won't get bored

When I am too tired to stand

I'll still praise Your name, for it is grand

I'll praise You on my knees

For it is You who holds the keys

To life, salvation, and joy

You make my life something to enjoy

I simply desire to know You more

I'll praise You lying on the floor

For it is You that I adore

You make my life something more

Glorify Your Name

Let me glorify Your name

My life will never be the same

After finding You

Praise and worship are all that I do

Your name is so great

You have forever changed my fate

I'll sing of Your glory and grace

I run as though it is a race

To tell the world about You

Because You made me new

Where should I start

You put joy in my heart

You're with me night and day

You're the God who has the final say

You're mighty and strong

You're never wrong

You're the warrior that fights by my side

You'll forever be my guide

You catch me when I fall

To You, I am so small

But, You love me anyway

You're with me night and day

You put the moon and stars in the sky

Forever I'll lift Your name on high

I'll love You till the day that I die

Thank You for forgiving my sins

You're the God who always wins

I love You more each day

Even when I am old and gray

I'll sing of Your mercy and grace

And how it shines in even the darkest place

My Greatest Love

Our journeys don't look the same because God gave us each a different story. It would be boring to live the same life as everyone else and have the same outcomes, talents, and flaws. Our stories are all different because God made each one of us unique. Each one of our lives is a love story where we meet and get to know our greatest love, God. God loves us all, but He gave us each a different love story. We bring our own love story just for Him. So, press in and learn to love Him more each day. He will pour out His love upon you in ways far greater than you can hope for or imagine. God's love is incredibly unique and divine. Pursue Him, and His love for you will be revealed more and more each day.

I Love You

Your love is the song that my soul sings

It's your grace that each day brings

You reveal the truths that are unseen

Your actions are never mean

Everyday You hold my hand

Your love is so grand

I need You more

Your love makes me soar

You bless me each day

I will never find enough words to say

How much I love You

There is nothing that I can do

To express the feelings of my heart

With You, I'll never part

I'll praise You each day

I never want to go astray

Crush on You

I have this love for God that's deep and real. However, I still get the heart flutters of new love. When I read the Bible, and there's a verse that speaks to my heart, or when a pastor or preacher is speaking, and their message feels like it was meant just for me, it makes my heart leap for joy. It's like when your crush turns and looks back at you. It makes my heart just melt with love for God.

Seeker of Souls

Immerse me in Your love and grace

You find me in even the darkest place

You hear every prayer

Your presence reminds me that You care

You wipe away every tear

You remind me not to fear

You're mightier than any weapon or foe

Your strength breaks every bow

You shield me from every fiery dart

From me You promised never to part

You avenge the weak

It's our heart that you seek

With love, You call our name

Your love is constant, it stays the same

We are sinners, but Jesus took our shame

He carried our cross, and took our blame

Your perfect, unfailing love chases us down

Jesus, the prince of peace wears the crown

Your love always prevails

It was shown at the cross with Jesus' nails

My God, please lead the way

I will trust You and obey

Teach me how to please You more

It's Your love that I adore

Teach me how to be more like You

I want to please You in all that I do

I surrender it all to You

Thank you for making me new

My Everything

You're in every breath that I take

You pick up the pieces of my heart

after each heartbreak

You hold my hand when I feel alone

You hear every utterance and groan

You wipe the tears from my cheeks

You're the one that my soul seeks

You're my peace

You make every enemy cease

You're the rock that I cling to

I'll praise Your name until my face turns blue

You're faithful, and You stay by my side

You'll forever be my guide

Your love soothes my soul

It is in You that I have been made whole

I will never go astray

Forever I will trust You and obey

The Lamb

Jesus becoming the sacrifice for our sins is such a foreign concept to many of us. It can be difficult to grasp the concept of a blood sacrifice for our sins. Jesus is often referred to as the sacrificial lamb, and many people know that Jesus surrendered his life and was crucified on the cross. However, understanding the significance of this can be challenging. It used to be common practice for people to offer sacrifices to God. These sacrifices were made to cover a person's sin. The Old Testament explains in detail what animals were considered acceptable offerings and how they needed to be slaughtered. To be regarded as an acceptable offering for God, the livestock needed to be healthy, whole, spotless, and perfect. Then the animal was sacrificed; this sacrifice covered a person's sin. The sacrifice did not cover all their sins and the sacrifice only covered past sins and needed to be done again after another sin was committed. Jesus exempts us from this process because he became the sacrifice for all of our sins. Jesus is the son of God, and he lived a life completely free from sin. Jesus also set the standard of how we are to live our lives. Jesus is a teacher, and he taught people how to live their lives with integrity. His teachings were considered radical because they differed from the cultural and social norms. Jesus called men to love their wives, which in this period was such a radical idea because women did not have rights, and they were not considered equal beings. Jesus spent his life teaching people about God and showing us how we are called to live our lives. Then Jesus chose to die on the cross; his body was broken, his blood was spilled, and his life was surrendered. Jesus did what we could never do. He was the perfect, spotless, blameless, sinless being who became the sacrifice for our sins. His death set us free from sin because it did not just cover our sins like a lamb's; instead He took them away, forgiving them all and broke the power of sin over us. We no longer have to come before God with an offering for our sins because Jesus already paid the price for every single sin. Jesus took on the role of the sacrificial lamb and paid the price that we could never pay. Before Jesus was crucified, we were all slaves to sin. Jesus paid the ultimate price to free us from sin, making our freedom blood-bought and paid for. This is such an expensive price to pay; no resource, commodity, or price tag can equate to the price of being blood bought by Jesus. God so loved the world that He gave His one and only son so that anyone who believes in him will not perish but have eternal life. God loves every person in this world so much that He chose to sacrifice His one and only son for us. God loves you so much and values you enough to sacrifice His son for your freedom. God loves you enough to give you free will. God gives us a choice to accept the blood of Jesus for our sins and then live in Heaven with Him when we die or reject the price that Jesus paid for our salvation and perish. God does not want you to perish; God wants you to choose Him. However, God is a gentleman who loves us so much that He does not force us to accept the price that Jesus paid for our salvation. God gave us free will with the desire for us to choose Him. God loves you more than I can ever begin to express or understand. God chose us, and He decided to sacrifice His son for our freedom and pay the price that we could never pay. No sin can separate you from God, and your soul can not be sold because it was bought on the day Jesus chose to lay his life down on the cross. Every day is a gift, another opportunity to choose or reject God. My best advice is to choose Him. He decided to love you before you were even born, and He continues to love you and waits patiently for you to choose Him each day. God pours out His perfect and unfailing love upon you daily, His blessings are innumerable, and His love is pure. I am not worthy, but I have the privilege to accept Jesus, and I am honored to choose and serve him every day of my life.

CPSIA information can be obtained
at www.ICGtesting.com
Printed in the USA
JSHW021943270623
43888JS00003B/173